INSTANT LIVES
& MORE

INSTANT LIVES & MORE

HOWARD MOSS

Drawings by Edward Gorey

The Ecco Press
New York

Text copyright © 1972, 1973, 1974 by Howard Moss
Drawings copyright © 1972, 1973, 1974 by Edward Gorey

All rights reserved
First published by The Ecco Press in 1985
18 West 30th Street, New York, N.Y. 10001
Published simultaneously in Canada by Stoddart,
a subsidiary of General Publishing Co., Ltd., Don Mills

PRINTED IN THE UNITED STATES OF AMERICA
Library of Congress Cataloging in Publication Data
Moss, Howard, 1922 –
Instant lives & more.
1. Biography–Anecdotes, facetiae, satire, etc.
I. Title.   II. Title: Instant lives and more.
PS3525.08638I57   1985   813'.52   85-1678
ISBN 0-88001-076-2 (pbk.)

Second Printing, 1985

For Eudora Welty and Reynolds Price

CONTENTS

As the World is sifted into Time's Archives,
And the Bee reduceth Honey in his Hives,
So do We make our little, instant Lives . . .

—St. Julian of Padua

LOUISA MAY ALCOTT

Louisa had had Concord. Still, she felt a sense of loyalty, dim to the point of evasiveness, toward Karen, Lupe, and Olga, her madcap sisters, in whose eyes attainment and sluggishness were so uncomfortably abed. They all seemed to be of the same age. How could that be? Louisa often wondered. There they were, messily engaged in another spontaneous fudge-making contest that had turned the front of the house a lively brown—Karen with her fierce talents as a sculptress, Lupe with her good looks and imperturbable manners, and Olga with her cooking ability and school-of-hard-knocks brilliance. Only Louisa among them had been educated. In fact, none of the other girls could read or write, though they were, in an amateur, outdated way, tremendous talkers. Lupe, inexplicably, spoke nothing but a Spanish demotic at best.

"I'd rather spend the day with my hamster than a night with the Alcott girls," Mr. Crockett, the postmaster, had said. He was later arrested as a firebug.

Yet in spite of Louisa's many local attachments—not the least of which was to Lance Ruefrue, the handsome fidget who lived next door—she felt it was time to go. The scope of her talents could not be measured on the small field of Concord's prejudices. And this—this was the last straw! *Little Men* had been condemned by the Library Vice Squad as "a vile pit of unseemliness for minds under twelve and a jungle of ugly sensuality for those thirteen and over . . ." Louisa, characteristically, had opted for confrontation and faced Mrs. Fortress-Rondeau, the squad chairwoman, on the steps of Caldecott High.

"Mrs. Fortress-Rondeau . . ." Louisa began.

"Don't speak to me, you disgusting girl," Mrs. Fortress-Rondeau replied. She swept past Louisa into her brougham where, drawing the curtains, she took a deep swig of Campho-Phenique, her one indulgence. (One year later, she was to meet a tragic death. Outraged by a passage in Tennyson, she attempted to expunge the offending lines with her soap eraser and died of apoplectic fury. In her extremity, she fell on top of her husband, a tiny mouse of a man, who perished in the attempt to aid her. A memorial statue, *The Arrival of the Gnomes at Kittyhawk,* a tribute to the

Rondeau family, still stands in the public square at Sodoma, Mass.)

"Little frump," Louisa shouted after Mrs. Fortress-Rondeau, anticipating, in the singular, the title of a novel she was never to finish. But her words were as wind-music and to no avail.

JANE AUSTEN

"Jane, your hair is awfully dry tonight," said Jane Austen's sister, as she toasted a marshmallow over the grate. Evening, like an overturned fish bowl, was falling over Sussex. The fire rose up in the mantel, like a gentleman. As malleable as she was limber, Malaprop, the maid, entered with the tea tray, curtsied, the tray carefully balanced in her hands, and paused. "Rise up," said Jane, tossing aside a galley of *Sense and Sensibility*. Outside, it was 1811.

"Another clever novel, Miss?" asked Malaprop. She eyed the dowdy pastries with a sickened eye. How *could* they?

"Cleverer by far than cook," said Jane, with asperity. She detested pastry, even when it was first rate, an encomium that could hardly be applied to the *mille feuilles* whose layers sagged one against the other, like a ruined house flayed by wet wind. The inanity of custard!

"If you got more royalties . . ." her sister started to say, and then bit her lip. "Not that I'm complaining," she added. "I'm in no position to complain."

"You have gauged your position precisely," Jane replied to her sister. "Though the accuracy of your assessment hardly acts as a restraining force."

"You're so wordy, Jane," said her sister. "No wonder you have trouble with men."

Smugness aside, the derogation the remark conveyed was not lost, of course, on Jane.

"My dear Cassandra," she said. "Why don't *you* polish off these mephitic sweetmeats—it would only make your figure the more bizarre. I have a deadline to meet, you know." And with that, Jane swept out of the room, the galleys trailing behind her like a bridal train devised by a couturier impaled upon typography.

But, in Life, there would be no bridal train for Jane Austen.

=≡≡=

JOHANN SEBASTIAN BACH

"Thunderation!" Magda exclaimed. She'd just climbed the one hundred and seventeen steps to the belfry. "Do you have to sit here and compose all day just to prove you're a Christian believer?" She dodged one of the bells that began to sway ominously. Another metallic, clangorous, deafening concert! Why couldn't they all just shut up and pray quietly, the way she did? All this singing and howling! This ostentatious clamoring about the Lord! Wasn't there more true religious feeling in baking a pie than in constantly proclaiming the glory of God? Yes, there was, she said to herself, as she set Bach's simple lunch down on the table next to the organ.

"Sardine and salt-smelt sandwiches again?" Bach

6

queried, his kindly face creased by genius and consternation. Sometimes he felt the iron hand of alliteration directed Magda's culinary impulses. Such as they were. Sometimes he felt nothing.

"I thought you liked them," she said, about to burst into tears. Her emotions were close to the surface, on the few occasions when they weren't on it.

"Ach," Bach said, "I was only joshing. Sardine and smelt are my favorite fish."

Actually, Bach was being polite. He was getting tired of Magda's unimaginative recipes. She was a sweet and devoted creature, but the lip-smacking sensualities and heady subtleties of the true gourmet were beyond her.

"How are the cantatas coming?" Magda asked. "I see you're up to No. 198—(*Trauer-Ode*)."

Bach smiled. "I have twenty-two mouths to feed, *meine Kleine*. Not counting my own."

"Ruppert Feinshting is waiting for his organ lesson," Magda replied. "And I have to get back to the kitchen. I hope you haven't forgotten that the Kappelmeister is coming for dinner tonight. You know how fussy *he* is."

"Tonight?" Bach asked, incredulously.

"We're having rabbit and rice and radishes and roast ram," Magda confided. And rats and ropes and riffraff and reefs, she went on compulsively, to herself. "Ruppert has written a prelude and fugue." *She* knew where to get the knife in.

"Tell him I will be down—in a day or two," the great composer riposted.

For a few moments, Bach's mind had been diverted by small talk. But once Magda was gone—he could hear her falling down all one hundred and seventeen steps— he leaped from the table to the writing desk. The great chords and giant sonorities of the opening of the

B-Minor Mass had just thundered through his head. What did it matter now whether the sandwiches had been smelt or not?

LUDWIG van BEETHOVEN

"So, you're dedicating it to *him*," Beethoven's nephew said, tossing the score aside and flinging himself onto the couch, no mean feat since he was a huge monolith of a boy and the couch was made of pre-stressed chenille. "I thought the next one was going to be for *me*."

Beethoven walked to the window. Outside, Bonn's rush hour was taking its toll. Groups of angry sanitation workers, flourishing canes, attacked the week's debris—mounting vileries of urban indulgence. Beethoven was sorry to see that, under the cover of twilight, a few elderly matrons were being jostled by loiterers. He turned back to face his nephew.

"Karl," he began, "public affairs take precedence . . . after all . . . Napoleon . . ."

"Oh, *well*, if you're going in for *names*."

There was something captive, cryptic, and Coptic about Karl. Though the furnace of his overheated imagination worked full-blast, no steam was visible on the panes of its greenhouse. What was to Karl the headache of reality was to Beethoven the migraine of the gods.

"Well, if I can't have a symphony, can I at least have a concerto?" Karl pursued.

Beethoven was touched by the boy's intensity, but as a "displaced parent," he thought it his duty to pile impediment in the way of ego. He remained silent.

"A quartet?"

Silence again.

"A few German dances?"

Though it hurt Beethoven more than it did Karl, the composer's lips remained sealed.

"A teensy bagatelle?"

The boy looked so crestfallen that Beethoven finally gave in.

"Oh, all right, Karl. The 33rd Piano Sonata."

Karl brightened—an effect of minimal luminosity.

"The four-hand xylophone arrangement, that is."

Karl rose. He felt he had at least got *some*thing.

"I have to go," he said. "I'm having a beer with Myerbeer." And he left, singing a few snatches of Mozart.

THE BRONTËS

The moon-sulphured lightning zigzagged across the moors. The weather spoke aloud—snare drum and kettle. It was the worst storm in Yorkshire's history. Charlotte sat in the schoolroom staring out the window, as if to be stamped by the landscape like a brand. Emily had just come down, afloat as from shipwreck. Total immersion. She had been working on "something"—*what*, Charlotte refused to ask. Might one consider Anne's lack of appearance an abeyance?

"He's imbibing again," Charlotte said. She bore the equine traces of spinsterhood with equanimity.

"It's the weather," Emily countered. "He really doesn't have enough to do."

"*Do?*" Charlotte was scornful. "What about the wainscoting? And the roof? And the drains?"

Emily paled. Anne entered the room with the elegance of a squatter.

"Hello," she said, lying down on the floor. "There's a leak in the drawing room."

"*Don't* be eccentric," Charlotte admonished.

"Is being comfortable eccentric?" Anne asked. "Is being *happy?*" She burst into tears and rushed from the room.

"Her devotional verses are going to her head," Charlotte said.

Her head? Emily thought. *Your* head.

"Where *is* he?" Charlotte went on.

"In the pantry. Estivating—if one considers summer a mitigation."

"*I* never have. Your twisting of language . . ."

Emily rose to draw the curtains. She turned and spoke as if she were addressing air. "Of course, if I'd wanted to write a *popular* novel . . ."

A thunderclap rendered human speech *de trop*.

"Shall we begin?"

"How *can* we without Branwell? This *weather,*" Emily complained.

"What's the weather got to do with it? *I* say that Heathcliff was *my* character, that I wrote his name down in this notebook four years ago." She brandished the named object. "You've been filching, sneaking, plagiarizing . . ."

Emily stiffened. "You know that's a lie."

Something terrible was happening to Charlotte. At last!

A flash of lightning revealed a figure swaying in the doorway. It was Branwell, intoxicated, menacing . . .

"Where's my grog?" he screamed. "Where's my filthy, blasted grog?"

Rain fell steadily on Haworth.

VITTORE CARPACCIO

"There are so few places that know how to serve a really delicious egg tempera," Mrs. Bronzino said, putting the dish down in front of her guest. Mrs. Bronzino was a plump dolphin of a girl, immune to paradox and insincerity.

"Another drink, Carpaccio?" Bronzino asked.

"Perhaps a bit more vermouth," Carpaccio rejoined. He was working on S. *Giorgio degli Schiavoni* and rarely had a chance to go out and meet people.

"It isn't often we painters and sculptors see each other anymore, is it?" Bronzino asked, a tear of recollection bronzing his eye. "We should meet more, talk over mutual problems . . ."

"Trade secrets, you mean?" Carpaccio asked, instantly deciding against it.

"No, not really," Bronzino responded. "Intramural seminars, I'd say—something personal, yet . . ."

"No one's eating anything," Mrs. Bronzino chimed in. "You can't stand on those scaffolds all day without some solid food."

Carpaccio looked down. His shoes were covered with muck. There was no doubt of it, Venice was going downhill—but why harp on it at a social occasion?

"You're doing wonderful things, Zino," he said. "I wish I had your mastery of perspective."

"And I your sweep and scope," Bronzino shot back.

"*Corso segundo,*" Mrs. Bronzino shouted, clearing away the table with her arm.

Carpaccio hesitated. "Is Caravaggio coming?" he

asked nervously as soon as Mrs. Bronzino was out of the room.

"Caravaggio? Here? On the same night as . . ." Bronzino stopped. He had gone too far.

"I *know* he's been here," Carpaccio said tensely. A trace of bitterness made his voice falter. "Why don't you have Verocchio? And the Carracis? The whole confusing bunch?" He began to tremble.

"The drink is going to your head, my friend," Bronzino kindly said. "It seems my wine is strong tonight," he continued. He was referring to the fourth of their party, Al Dente, the restorer, who was lying under the table.

"Basta! Pasta!" Mrs. Bronzino shouted, hurling herself through the doorway with a huge tray of spaghetti.

"Forgive my outburst," Carpaccio said to Bronzino. "I have suffered much."

"I know, I know," Bronzino responded. "Bernini hasn't made it easy for me, either. But remember this —Caravaggio's first name is . . . Michelangelo!"

"What a headache *that*'s going to be in the years to come," Carpaccio said. And they fell to like hungry bears discovering honey.

FRÉDÉRIC CHOPIN

The Majorcan afternoon, streaked like a tomato tulip, enveloped the island in a beneficent blaze. Each stunted tree seemed to thrust itself up with a pert starchness, and the sea, glinting irremediably in the distance, added a touch of the mysterious to what was already a mystery. Would the "Prelude" ever come right? Chopin thought, his fingers idly straying across the keyboard. The piano was out of tune, as usual. The dampness of the island had turned the strings into veritable nerves—nerves sensitive to the slightest change in pressure, the merest alteration in the alchemy of water density. Suddenly, she was on the stairs, standing there looking down at him, the whole force of her figure concentrated in one galvanizing full-length portrait.

"Why don't you cough more, Frédéric," she said. "Then I could stay up the *whole* night." Slowly she descended the stairs. He stared at her.

"*Again?* You're going to be like this *again?*"

"I don't know what you're talking about," she replied. "Dolcilita has prepared breakfast?" Her Spanish, he noted with envy, was improving. It was still light-years away from the Castilian glitter.

"Am I supposed to run the house, *too?*" Frédéric asked, and instantly regretted it. It could just possibly be true.

In truth, they were getting on each other's nerves. Little had George Sand reckoned what it would mean to be sequestered in a house on an island with someone who played the piano more than half the day. Its tinkle, as she referred to it, had become abhorrent to her. She was afraid that, finally, she would come to detest music, even really *serious* composers like Massé and Tagliafico. Besides, *François le Champi* was going badly. That was something she could never admit to him—she felt her powers were failing. Alas, what lack of communication exists even among the great! For her fear was, *au fond,* his fear as well. He could compose now only in the key of A minor—he who had once been the sovereign of B flat major, who had had every nuance of the scale so firmly under his finely pointed fingertips that it had been said of him, "Chopin breathes B flat major." He was no ordinary Pole.

"Dolcilita!" George Sand shouted, but her voice

17

was drowned out by a louder sound. Someone was insistently pounding on the door. They were united now in a common fear. Could it be her publisher? Or *his?*

CLAUDE DEBUSSY

The rowboat tilted again, and he slid past the gun-
wales, almost unconscious, the score still tightly
clutched in his fist. His head knocked against an oar—
thank God the oars were still there!—and he made a
feeble effort to fasten it. He had been sick, he esti-
mated, for four hours. And still there was no sight of
land! What an idiot he had been to eat nothing but
fish for two weeks in the hope that it would make his
internal organs marine, that the rhythms and fabrics
of the sea would drench him completely! When he'd
called the doctor on the twelfth day—he'd been feeling
queasy—the doctor had said, "Not *salt*-water fish,
Claude. *Fresh.*" He had bungled everything. Were the

bilges working? Dimly, he could see, scrawled on top of the manuscript score, a few words above the notes. *De l'aube à midi sur mer* (From dawn until midday on the sea). Or was it the second movement, *Jeux des vagues* (Play of the waves)? The score danced before his eyes. He closed them. The boat was lifted by a wave. He was going to be sick again.

How he longed to be back working on *Prélude à l'après-midi d'un faune!* Then he had simply lived among the goats in the backhills of Sicily for a month, his flute never far from his mouth, his foot never far from his flute. He had allowed the Italian summer heat to penetrate to his very bones—the sensuality of those sun-drenched months, dimly felt even now, caused a feeble smile to cross his overly sensitive lips. His beard was *embrumé* with salt. The whole project was a mistake. He was beginning to hate the sea. "I hate it," he said. "I really *hate* it."

He closed his eyes once more and drifted helplessly. The awful scene that had occurred when he returned from Italy flashed into his mind. He had entered the blue sitting room of the house in Paris; his wife had looked up. She was seated at her *flânerie*, sewing; half a rose wound its way, hopefully, through her hoop.

"*Est-ce que les choses vont bien?*" she queried. And then she had burst into tears, cried bitterly and childishly, the way Mélisande would cry, six years later, at the Opéra, and bring the audience (the half of it that stayed to see the work to its finish) to its feet.

Would the boat never stop rocking? His mind was beginning to wander.

The *Children's Corner Suite* was behind him; the *Études* were still to come.

EMILY DICKINSON

As the twilight gathered around her, Emily sat at the window and looked out at Amherst, a small, silent town, wrought up, here and there, into gables. Like its lean cemeteries, its sense of scale was small but neatly done. A hunchback, made sinister by dusk, hobbled off toward the local; the bar at *The Lord Jeffrey* was doing a bang-up business as usual. Amherst was no Araby of dazzling transports but the icicle-blue needle of true North. Emily sighed. How secondary the primal can become, she thought. Poetry, which she had taken up to disguise the "operation," now absorbed her completely. Though the illegal manufacture of witch hazel in New England could be laid solely at her door, she was, to the world at large, "the wallflower sonneteer"—a misnomer on two counts.

She took a sip of dandelion wine from the fluted Waterford goblet on the windowsill. Across the way, the Reverend Hodgson was raising his hat. She bowed slightly, her lace shawl shirred about her birdlike shoulders—spinster but also ruthless businesswoman, as the sailors sweating off the Rhode Island coast knew all too well. At this very moment, they were pumping barrel after barrel full of witch hazel distilled from her secret formula. She had swallowed the "recipe" at the tense meeting in the cave near Mt. Holyoke when Rudolph Moselle, the wine merchant, threatened to wrest it from her by force. Only *she* knew the ingredients. And she had elected silence. That white sepulchral thing. Even the pirates had cheered.

She still had a taste for "the hazel," which surprised her, considering the gallons she'd consumed. A line suddenly sprang into her head: "I taste a hazel never brewed . . ." She rushed over to her writing desk, an affair so elaborate it had come all the way from Boston. How many lines she had lost simply by thinking she would remember them! "Brewed in . . . ?" She bit the end of her pencil. She had so little time. She would spend half the night at the window waiting for the signal—a broomstick hoisted over Amherst's gym—that would let her know that the second ship, loaded with "it," had departed for Portugal. "Brewed in Portugal?" No. Barrels? That was it! "I taste a hazel never brewed/ In barrels . . ." Barrels . . . what? Ah, she had it! Swept by brine! "In barrels swept by brine." No, that wasn't right, either. Brewed? Bars? Taverns? "I taste a hazel never brewed/ In taverns ripped by toil"? "On tabbards scooped in oil"? She was getting away from the subject. Or was the subject getting away from her?

The original was better: "I taste a hazel never brewed/ In barrels scooped in brine . . ." Or was it "stewed in brine"? She looked down at the paper. The crucial verb was the one word she hadn't written down!

The signal! She was forgetting the signal!

She dashed back to the window just in time to see the broomstick hoisted against the sky. *That,* at least, was accomplished. But in regard to the poem, she knew, now, the terrible task of revision that lay ahead.

JOHN DONNE

If you would do what John Donne did,
You merge the Clergy with the Id.

This recently discovered couplet, found in the famous sewing basket unearthed during the recarpeting of Carlyle's hall, was first attributed to Crashaw and then to Vaughan by Dr. Rennselaer, whose "original" but logically absurd work, *Was Crashaw Vaughan?* (Salt Press, Epsom, New Hampshire, 1958), produced a faint ripple of conjecture in the academic community in the late fifties. The early puzzlement and dismay that greeted the couplet's publication seems, in retrospect, inexplicable at best, and, at worst, a deliberate act of obfuscation. In an earlier study of mine, *Death and Donne* (Mercier Dental School Mimeographs, Steeple, Kansas, 1959), I refuted Dr. Rader's simplistic contention that "it might well be a forgery, of unknown origin." [1] Recent carbon tests—carried out, many professionals feel, with an ineptness that suggests equivocation—left the matter moot, but a sense of *tone,* if nothing else, should have made it obvious to even the most rudimentary of scholars that the two lines could have been written by none other than "the swart strutter of Cheyne Walk." [2] It is the simple purpose of this paper to show that internal evidence proves conclusively that Donne was the author of this important, and I have no hesitation in saying major, find.

The *jeu d'esprit* of the lines—one need hardly mention their metrical *buoyancy*—tells us much about what the future Dean of St. Paul's was thinking as a cavalier young man. They combine deeply felt religiosity, humor, and outspoken sensuality. If we look more closely at the couplet, we see still another strain: a cabalistic exploration of syntax, daring yet magnificent in its reverberations, for the verb "do," with its primary meaning of "to make, fabricate, or create," as well as its overt sexual connotations, is brilliantly exploited in the scatological puns "do," "done," and "did," the second term in the series being a homonym of the author's name, an example, if one were still needed, of the metaphysical cunning that turns so many of Donne's poems, with their coarse, cross-bred rhythmical structures, into what Dr. Johnson referred to as "the rest home of the caesura." [3]

In his use of the future pluperfect, Donne emphasizes the ghost of the negative by the very assertion of the positive, an inversion felt rather than sounded in "Donne did" (done did) with its corollary implication "don't do" (don't do). To underline the internal rhymes of "you," "do," and "you," and their almost imperceptible repetition in the "Do . . ." of "Donne," would, in my opinion, not only pile Pelion on Ossa but thrust insult in the face of inscrutability.

[1] Rader, Gloria, *The Metaphysical Mop-Up,* Litmus Pamphlets, Tulsa, 1954.
[2] *Chain Songs for the Guitar,* Boozy & Hawks, New York, 1958.
[3] Anonymous, *Call Girl to Dr. Johnson,* Ithaca Broadsides, Auburn, 1972.

SERGEI EISENSTEIN

One more heavy lunch at the Winter Palace, and he thought he'd go mad. But there was Klotz-Vronsky to placate, and Grubov, in order to see the rushes, and, for technical reasons, Schrenkov, the Commissar of Filters. He would never finish *Kremlin Bells,* not at the rate they were going. The few Westerners familiar with the uncut version smuggled into Mexico say it resembles a remake of *Sunset Boulevard* seen from the pool's point of view.

"Sergei? A little tea?"

Nadya smiled at him, the dyed blonde hair swinging with ferocious coquetry in a huge pigtail behind her.

She lifted the samovar. Teapot or weapon? He was never sure. Too old to be a soubrette, she was not too old to do a little character acting for the OGPU.

"Enchanté, Nadya," he heard himself saying. "You look as good as ever." He was determined not to lie. In truth, Nadya was a workhorse who had caught the first faint whiff of the glue factory.

"They are saying . . ."—Nadya's standard beginning, always with its veiled threat—". . . they are saying that bourgeois influences are making Soviet film a smokescreen behind which the worker's real interests are being distorted and corrupted." Her smile was hideous now. "What do you think, Sergei?"

"Well," he muttered, avoiding the stream of boiling water she carefully directed toward his foot, "There's a great deal to be said on *both* sides. The way of darkness is the way of light." He swallowed a macaroon—the macaroon of his undoing? Bah! He was being melodramatic!

She spat her words out with contempt: "Capitalist provocateurs are attempting to gain the minds of the people through images. We must stop them. No images. Just facts." Nadya was panting heavily as she finished. Sergei wondered idly what conviction did to the lungs.

"But a fact *is* an image, Nadya, as I think the great Russian people, in their endless struggle to replace necessities with luxuries, would agree."

Nadya was wearing a voluminous skirt. Somewhere in all those folds, another reel of film lay coiled. Could he get it before she exposed herself—and *it*?

"Delicious tea," he said. "But no *lemons*?" His tone was rakish. "Ah, there they are! Down there!" And he pointed to a plate under the table that one of his dis-

27

ciples had placed there, the night before, under the cover of darkness.

She bent down. In an instant, the film was in his hand, then in his capacious shopping bag.

"Do you have a little part for me, Sergei?" Nadya begged, as she straightened up and turned round. "I am not *completely* against *montage*."

They looked at each other. All that had happened between 1905 and the October Revolution lay between them.

"But of course, my dear," he said. "I was just about to ask you."

Which is why Nadya appears, for an eighth of a second, in Reel 3 of *Kremlin Bells*, rather unbecomingly, as the Second Piano Tuner.

FORD MADOX FORD

Her coldness, a form of abatement, struck him at once. Chagrin, that ignoble branch of pity, stirred in his breast. *Had* he misused the girl? There were so many times when the reverse seemed the case, so many mornings when he woke with the half-disabused feeling that he had been possessed by an image rather than a material being—eidolon without flesh, avatar sans features —and yet, her sensuality, when they were together, struck him as a palpable force and made his trepidations seem half real and half absurd.

"You were saying?" he asked.

She looked at him with the aristocratic hauteur of the innocent. *Was* she innocent? Or was she the servant of a degeneracy so deep that its carrier was unaware of the disease that formed her very substance?

"Nothing, really," she murmured. The brim of her hat cast a pencil-line of shadow across the fine grillwork of the railing. The smell of fresh water, of the spring river struggling to give forth its scent, suddenly assailed his nostrils. She *was* lovely. Of that there could be no doubt.

"Nothing at all?" he pursued. His uniform seemed to him stale and officious. It seemed to her pale and unpropitious.

"Oh, I suppose it's a matter of viewpoint," she countered, ambiguously.

"The war, you know. It's done something to all of us." His face was serious.

She looked at him in surprise. "What war?" she asked.

"You don't mean . . ." he began, astonished.

"You're trying to frighten me," she went on. "Just because . . ."

"Just because . . . what?"

"I don't know," she responded.

"But my uniform. Surely . . ."

"I thought you just . . . dressed up."

"Dressed *up?*"

"Or *down,* possibly," she added, with contempt.

"What do you mean?" he asked, sensing a reversal in their positions.

"Oh, Ford, *really!*" And she stamped her well-shod foot against the brick of the causeway. Back in the trenches, it was the one solid thing he was to remember of that long afternoon.

PAUL GAUGUIN

In spite of his increasing insanity, he still made a good husband, Sheila thought, as she raised the blind overlooking the abattoir. And after all, how many times did a girl like *her* marry a stockbroker like *him?* She came from a small Danish farm whereas he came from a big French city. He was highly sophisticated as well as well off. And what Sheila really cared about was a home, nice clothes, good food, so she could hold her head up in a crowd, particularly the fast crowd they had started going around with recently. She wondered if she measured up, if Paul really loved her. *Really*

really. Quick tears came to Sheila's eyes, tiny as they were. "Oh, I'm being a sentimental fool," she mused. "I'm always this way before I have my Pernod."

She passed Paul's huge experimental painting of a Maori nude asleep in a mangrove grove, beset by flowers. "Ugh," Sheila said, involuntarily. She hated all that stuff. As soon as she walked into the kitchen, she saw the note lying on the table. *"Qu'est-ce-que c'est?"* she asked herself out loud. It read: "Sheel: Hate to have to tell you this but Vince and I have left for Tahiti irredeemably. Marriage and the whole middle-class *shtick* is not for me. Take care of Bunny, Lapsie, Gorgon, and Iseult. I left ten francs for you on one of the tables at *La Flore*. Paul."

Sheila slumped to the floor, and it was only because a neighbor, hearing the terrific thud—described, to the press, as "a veritable thunderclap"—came in and found her that she survived. Days later, waking up while the nuns bathed her wrists with cognac, she became hysterical, and, in fact, it took several years for Sheila to recover fully. Though she eventually remarried, she only became reconciled to Paul's desertion at the huge Gauguin retrospective of 1946, when, as an old woman, she tottered up the steps of the Louvre to receive the "Old Wives Award," one of France's most coveted decorations, for the many faithful years she had spent as the first, and only legitimate, wife of Paul Gauguin, immortal painter of the South Seas.

EL GRECO

"Why not make a virtue out of a defect, El?" the kindly eye doctor asked, bending over the artistic boy. Or should it be "autistic," the doctor thought to himself. The boy's eyes were not only hopelessly astigmatic, but a peculiarity, unique to the doctor's experience and probably genetic in origin, had elongated the lenses of the irises so that El Greco saw every object in the world attenuated to the point of emaciation. It was as if some abstract giant had pulled the taffy of reality out as far as it would stretch from both ends simultaneously, and then let it snap. The boy was his own distorting mirror and his life would be either a perpetual fun fair or . . . a horror show.

"Virtue out of a defect? Do you think I *can*, Dr. Visione?" El Greco responded eagerly. He was only twelve at the time.

"Indeed I do," Dr. Visione said, and he handed El Greco a stick of the Byzantine candy, *Muerte del dolci* (variously translated as "death from sugar-sweetness" and "the sweetness unto the death"), a favorite of children at the time.

Years passed and El Greco had almost forgotten the incident, especially since he no longer thought of his difficulty as a defect. In fact, he was proud of it for it was the source of his unique vision of the universe. Why should everybody be alike? His paintings had gained notoriety, and he was not far behind. The only person still unconvinced of his greatness was Inez Miguelez, the gypsy dancer who had aroused his ardor. Of scant stature—some claimed she had been deliberately miniaturized by evil forces—she danced like mercury on tabletops. Too tiny to chin up under her own steam, many is the night the exquisite hands of the genius painter, El Greco, were used merely as a kind of hydraulic lift to get Inez from under the table, where she was so often found, to the top of it, where she was so often left.

"I am Flamenco through and through," Inez kept repeating. But because she was so small no one could hear her.

In Spain, the Church and the State are one. The authorities wanted El Greco's paintings—they were their chief weapon in the long battle they were waging against the secularization of art (*el segulizionariola del arte*)—but they insisted that Inez must go.

El Greco and the authorities clashed.

Six months later, Inez became the tiniest nun in Spain.

ALDOUS HUXLEY

Penelope left a mark on St. Gaudin's that might more
accurately be described as a scar. Derision, coldness, the
absolute disdain of second-year goddesses, bespectacled
or Vampire, made not the slightest. Under her hands,
a mediocre hockey team became a dazzling instrument
of personal power; the Coffee Club, all Kensington
starch when she arrived, vibrated with Brazilian pro-
tein at the end—one could almost *smell* the beans. She
was energy incarnate. It was all the more amazing in
view of her appearance. Not a clue. She looked, actually, as if she were about to be ravished by an interior
decorator. The shoe was on the other foot. And what

freshgirl had ever before fallen desperately in love with the most famous taxidermist of his time? How many mornings she had dawdled in front of his shop, Della, her best friend, in tow! There Tony was, clear as a picture, ravishing as one, standing at work in his window. Never a nod for *them*. Had she fallen merely for window dressing? Or should one, in this case, say "stuffing"? That he did his extraordinary work in Barnstable-on-Weir instead of London only added to his inaccessibility.

"I can't *stand* it," she would rage at Della in Mrs. Moriarty's Tea Shoppe. "Oh, Della!" And Della, like a satellite moved by the emotions of the sun, would burst into tears. Would Penelope ever finish her term paper—"Adjectival Color in 'Crome Yellow' "—*now?*

She did meet Tony, finally, over crumpets at the Shoppe. She was looking remarkably well, devastating in kohl-dust, a bit of glitter. She knew his schedule to the second, knew even the dates of shipment of his glue, stays, string, kapok, and mattress ticking. She fell out of her chair onto his. "*So* sorry!" They stayed not at Barnstable's little inn but raced out in his Lancia to the shore. The Credenza Arms happily accommodated them. The Credenza Arms was all accommodation. "Happy?" Tony asked, looking down at her peach breasts, her movietone legs, the blonde swirl of hair, her smile a solid snowstorm. He was Italianate. "Delirious."

That was in March. By the time the jonquils had applied for their annual discounts, things were abroil. "He's been horrible, just horrible, Dell!" Disillusionment brought tears; her mascara ran obliquely from the four angles of her eyes. She resembled Greek statuary before it has been restored.

They had it out in his flat where she accused him of running a "waxworks"—a fatal mistake. To call his tiny chic museum a "waxworks" was to confuse Sissingham with St. John's Wood. She cried.

"How disgusting!" He walked toward his balcony. Then onto it.

"Tony . . ." The voice came at him like a vine making one last feeble effort to hoist itself up yet another inch of string.

"Yes?"

"Couldn't we . . . ?"

"Never." The habitual hoarse honey of his voice had gone coarse with irritation. "I'll take you back."

In his bathroom, she thought wildly of suicide for an instant. Instead, she carefully put on her silver mascara, then a gorgeous, generous streak of lipstick. Mauve. "I'm still beautiful," she said to the mirror. "I'm young. Younger." And she ran out, and out the door of the living room.

"Penelope! . . . Penelope! . . ." he called after her. She felt free.

"Taxi!" she cried. And *this* time there was no "dermist" after it.

HENRIK IBSEN

A spasmodic of prefilthied snow plummeted past the window. The frozen fishnet of Oslo, diamonded by stars, lay before his studio, a study in deadness. Only the fire provided any sense of movement; and for that, he was grateful. The studio was on a height near the port but the usual sound of the fishermen, the occasional foghorn, the shouts and songs that roared from the water all the summer long were absent. All was frozen into a frightening silence. Only the leaping fire stimulated his imagination. And that, it seemed, was not enough. Something dreadful was happening to the most preeminent playwright in Europe.

"What, what, what is wrong?" he asked himself, as if he were a stutterer. Should he take out the letter from Shaw again, those pages of praise that might restore his self-confidence? Or the note, somewhat ambiguous, from Wagner? Of course, he knew Chekhov despised his work. So what? What did the merely melancholy Russians know of the Northern sickness, the Northern anguish, the Northern *poison?* True, they were snow-blue, too, but what a vast gulf separated their vodka and samovars and violins from the icy gaieties and cold depths of the Scandinavians? He must forget Chekhov's comment; he must remember Shaw's. That was the pass he had come to.

He had used them all up, the themes. He had *done* women's rights, and syphilis, and waterworks, and power. He had done the neurotic woman feeding herself on the artist, destroying them both in the process. (He must not, today of all days, think of H. . . .

Wherever she was, he hoped she was suffering horribly, suffering the way she had made half of Oslo suffer. What a fool he had been to write *A Doll's House!* It had only given her an excuse to walk out on him!)

He thought of topics, but they slipped from his mind almost as soon as they formulated themselves. Bear-baiting? No, no, that was in another country, and besides, the bear . . . Alcoholism? He reached for the beer that, it seemed, had become his one solace. It was 5:00 A.M. and he'd already gone through eight cases! The misuse of lumber? The smuggling in of wigs? If he could only think of something that would capture the imagination of the young! They were the ones who went to the theater *these* days. Vanity presses?

He sat up with a start. The suffering of audiences! That was it! And he began *Peer Gynt* at once.

HENRY JAMES

He took a dim view, if, indeed, a view, in all conscious-
ness, could be considered one, when the very act of its
perception was, by definition, barely discernible, of
biography, that addiction to "truth-seeking" that so
often cloaked, when it did not, more accurately, *mask*,
a predilection for poking into corners best left un-
poked, for lifting up stones heavy enough, one would
have thought, to crush existence itself out of the low
and wriggling forms of life that secreted themselves,
ever so hopefully, ever so persistently, in pursuit of a
safety indubitably not to be vouchsafed, beneath the
mossy sides of their seemingly permanent shelters.
Poor worms to be so disabused! And, by analogy, poor
diaries of the spirit to be so wrenched out of darkness!
That he, the author of *What Maisie Knew*, should be
asked to offer sacrifices at the altar of a God he did not

worship, neither as communicant nor convert, to act, doubly the slave, as the servitor of Mammon, a "deal" —as the American traders, ever hot in the pursuit of profit, might say—seemed to him not only to rub salt into an old wound but to be a special form of affront, as insulting as if, laid hands on by the misinformed, a first edition were to be used merely for the swatting of flies. He would not, no, though he needed, God knows, the "cash," needed it to water, as it were, the fine inter-meshing network of his creative locks and canals, needed it for passages over water made humdrum by cargo boats prosaically labeled food, clothing, and shelter, do it. He, Henry James, write a biography? Oh, he had done one once, a long time ago, that long dull book he need not ever think about again, that monument to industry, that hazard of profit, but—he addressed his mirror—this was something else again, *this* was a different case, a flogging of the mind, an embarrassment to the spirit, a deliberate, could it be, *rudeness,* on the part of his publishers because the plays had failed? The truth was he could not write the book. He did not, to put the fact as broadly and as sim-ply as possible, know who Leon Edel was.

JAMES JOYCE

Being a broth of a poi, cod-lei but Chile, to whom
Doubloom seized to half charm, eggs isle seemed puf-
ferable. He Christ the Iris zei, he crossed the Ingres
flannel and maid his weigh a broad. Zoo rich! Elps!
EEEEEEEEEEk! Them Swiss miss misses me. Watch
out, Montaignes, and them Edel (Weiss) Leon? Ted?
Price? Ah, my Tyne is come, said the looney.
    —Been around, Fin a Goon? the sty shun Master
asked.
    —Oops und din, neary and farry, dune and ma-
rooned, the sly fix respun dId.
    Thar she wuz, his foot your beride! Dumb in a
comb, she cum in a dream, Yanna! Plura see, plura
bull, pal a Sade, plura Belle! His Rhine stone, his dime
monde, his night *mer!*
    He halteringly two-tempt to smote in smell talk.
    —How river, Larry? Diego Rivera? Miss Issippi?
    —Hud, son, she swimmingly stood. Ah, sea side,
Smelt auk?
    —Small talc, he ably Ripe Post Ed.
    We drawers the curt Teen ova the seen. Suffers to
say, soon they wuz sloping to bedden, slopping to bide
in, inseys and outseys, Adams and Eves. And sometimes
a mat in the nay. He Shake-speared. She marsh-Mar-
lowed. They Ben to the Jon, son. He stang in his path:
Can't Elbe Liffey dat Mann of mien.
    —Z larffed, Bayou bist mir Seine. Bra bra! Throw
another wreck-word on the Vico.
    Minus the slightest idea of a didie, they doe mess
tick, night Afton nit après nought, lunch on, dindin,

café, lay. Heaven a Bull? A food dime was Hades by hell.

Minnary and Massary, a loon and a lambey, their childerness lighted like snow. A Livery delivery! Right on Thames! Evil, alive, and lo!

Yanna wassail. Pill? Oh! Sick dick was dockery two.

Don dye, our heros childer cry. Out went Yanna onto the river Styx and bones onto the stream of the dream Don down, the donney and bonney bonbon farther and father to fjord to shore to Norway more to see no more a broth of a poi Being . . .

ZOLTÁN KODÁLY

Zoltán Kodály manifested his musical ability at an early age by singing and humming. Often his fingers would run back and forth across an imaginary keyboard. "What is Zoltán doing with his hands?" the peasants would ask. The mystery was soon cleared up when a piano was brought from a neighboring town and Zoltán whisked through a few early Haydn sonatas he had been secretly studying in the barn. He was shunted from one conservatory to another and finally sent to

Russia, where he studied "Chords" in St. Petersburg and "Tunes" in Moscow. A short course in "Oriental Chimes" at a remote outpost in Siberia completed his musical education.

His middle period is characterized by exquisite folk songs popular both with the layman and the musical connoisseur—songs such as *Peas in Your Bonnet, Why Does the May Queen Beat Her Ward?* and *Home Lights,* perhaps the most famous of all. (After its first performance, Béla Bartók said, "It has the ring of inauthenticity.") Kodály's song cycle, *Windings,* was succeeded by a more tightly organized group of songs, *Bindings,* with the texts supplied by the leading poets of the day.

His one opera, *Short Order Cook of the Night,* based on the Osiris legend, was a failure, and was hissed off the stage in Moldavia.

He led an undramatic life and was married late to a former student, Serbia Smith, a butterfat tester. They traveled narrowly over the years and came to the United States where they gave a series of joint recitals marred by personal bickering. On his American tour, Kodály introduced a new group of songs that included the rousing *Hideabout* and the drowsier *The Sleep of the Seven Droners.*

He held various organ posts over his lifetime but was forced to give them back by an act of the Hungarian Parliament.

T. E. LAWRENCE

Because his mother had been humiliated at a Council Meeting, Lawrence suffered a life of emotional deprivation. Its symptoms were many and frequent: inane fitfulness, a disquieting habit of kneeling at pig fairs, and a tendency to disrobe in the face of authority. Thought of as "daft" by his peer group, he was forced to change schools. Yet even at Oxford, an outsider impelled toward farther and farther perimeters, he found it difficult to make friends. All the more reason to wonder at the towering achievement of *Omar*, that miraculous distillation of the East, not yet available to the general reader, which I have had the privilege of fingering in the cafeteria of the British Museum. I found it a work deeply intolerable and without the sweep of his epic study of Bedouin life, *Land, Sand, Soil, and Oil.* The intervening years spent overlooking a coke pit have never been sufficiently chronicled, but now, due to the deaths of Pastor Fielding and his wife, Mercy—both of whom stupidly drank rusty water—the story can at last be outlined.

Before embarking for the Arabian Peninsula, Lawrence spent ten years running an underground bakery, The Gnomic Cupcake, at Botched Riding. (Reginald Corby claims in *Separate Cover* that Lawrence's efforts as a pastry cook were financed and directed by the Foreign Office.) His later life as a sheepherder has been too well documented in Cicely Shearing's *Sleeping with Sheep* for me to repeat the bare facts here. By the time Lawrence arrived in Arabia, he was wearing a pair of imbued boots made from the end papers of remaindered novels. He stepped off the bus to the wild cheers of nomadic chieftains who, mistaking his boots for sacred objects, extended homage. It was only the first of many misunderstandings that were to turn Arabia into a colorful battlefield.

After several bloody fights, including his courageous retreat from one oilfield to another, Lawrence returned home where, informed that he was about to become a legendary figure, he succumbed in a bike accident.

FRANZ LISZT

"Please, Marie!" Franz shook his locks in anger. Didn't she realize that, sitting on the keyboard, she made arpeggios impossible? This was not the first time she had interfered with his work. "Off, off," Liszt cried.

"You sound like a dog," Marie countered. "All work and no play . . ."

A blow cleaved the brilliance of the remark.

"Franz!" Marie mouthed in astonishment. But he was too busy inventing the symphonic poem to turn around.

That afternoon, over a double consommé soggy with disunion, Liszt asked, "Where's Cosima?"

Marie's brow darkened. "Where indeed! One minute she's with von Bülow, the next with Wagner . . ."

"I told you not to mention that man's . . ."

"All right, all *right*. You asked." Marie got up from the table. She was heavy with child again. Where will it end? Liszt asked himself, preparing for another whirlwind tour of the musical centers of Europe: Lannion, Vaasa, and Bruges. Getting the piano up on the horses was not the least of his difficulties. At Liszt's approach, the horses would pretend to be musical and stamped out tunes with their hooves. And then, he was fussy about clothes. Should he take the black? The blue? Marie was very little help despite her liberal views.

Later, as kapellmeister at Weimar, he began his liaison with Princess Carolyne von Sayn-Wittgenstein.

"Sayn," he said one day. "What do you think of this?"

And hers were the first ears ever to hear the jellylike strains of the *Liebestraum*.

Another frantic tour of the minor spas of Hungary, marked everywhere by screaming teenage Hungarian girls attempting to overturn his barouche, made Liszt think of retirement.

"Shall I?" he asked a talented pianist he was tutoring. *"Que penses-tu,* Dierdre?"

"Dunno," Dierdre mumbled, going back to her Czerny without a pause. It was difficult since she was sitting on the keyboard and could hardly sight-read at best.

But the images of secular life had begun to fade for Liszt, and he received his orders as an abbé in 1865. He was surprised when he opened them because they simply read, *"Please* don't compose any more Hungarian Rhapsodies."

GUSTAV MAHLER

(For Luchino Visconti)

On the lively train racing between Florence and Rome, Gustav sat reading *Death in Venice*. The story seemed strangely familiar, even chillingly so, and as he turned toward the window he saw reflected in its pane the face of Flaglio Czerneck, the Italian Pole, staring at him intently, the way he had stared all those months at the pension in Bologna. The slim, cold-cream flute of his youth, the serene comitas of his brow suggested a lily preserved in snow in some alpine ravine situated at an unimaginable height. Gustav had gone to Bologna to recover from a mental breakdown and, for two years, he had been under the care of the world-famous hospital aide, Dr. Bruckner. As Gustav's depression had left him, his sense of the grandiose had increased. Now, in the womb of his attaché case, another masterwork lay

51

unborn whose score made demands on the chorus never dreamed of before in the history of music. Why *not* a symphony, finally, with all the Italian boys in the world drafted to sing its intricate canons?

He met Flaglio's insistent eyes in the train window again. They were deepset, olive, almond-shaped, and filmed—perhaps because of the long hours Flaglio spent on his manuscript of Polish prayers and petitions. The translation was to be published, he dreamed, under the title of *Prayers and Petitions from the Polish*. And set to music, perhaps, by G . . . . v M . . . . r?

Was the artist a criminal at heart, or was it the other way around, Gustav pondered? He couldn't be sure. Maybe that was the reason all Vienna had laughed at the premiere of his opera, *Rumpelstiltskin*. Flaglio abruptly got up, and, with a gesture one part Pole and two parts Italian, summoned Gustav to follow. As he stumbled forward to the next car, Gustav gasped—Flaglio was heading for *bagaglio!*

Gustav, who had eaten nothing all day because of the chickenpox epidemic that was transforming Italy into a vast funeral parlor, rose halfway from his seat. And then he felt it—a sickening, maddening desire. Only one thing could slake it. Chicken salad! Perhaps the most dangerous dish of all, considering the weather, Italy's ambivalent attitude toward mayonnaise, and the infestation of the salad worm (*lingi pustata*) that had made celery the most fought-over legume of the Mediterranean. The train plunged into a tunnel. Under the cover of darkness, Gustav grabbed a fistful of chicken salad from a neighboring table, to the angry surprise of a large Sicilian family. Though the club car was soon a shambles, it was a decisive moment in the history of nineteenth-century Western symphonic music.

SOMERSET MAUGHAM

In Benares, one can distinguish the Mandarin from
the maverick by a simple test. After the rain stops and
the heat hangs heavy, the children come by with a
drink called jahda, which they sell for a tuppence or
two. Made of papaya and mint, it seems irresistibly
cool. Consumed in any amount over four ounces, it
actually increases body temperature by twelve degrees.
Those who have not been in India long invariably buy
it and drain the small container to the dregs. Old India
hands know better. In the monsoon season, one drinks
nothing, as a matter of fact, between sunrise and sunset. The period of waiting is known as "thirstlight."

Millicent Carterhalf had had seventeen ounces of
jahda and was perspiring profusely as she faced Colo-
nel Fitzroy across the bridge table at the Club. "Can a
slattern really be a good bridge player?" Fitzroy asked
himself as he dealt out the cards. Fitzroy had been the
most colorful member of the 16th Hussars Dragoons
and had faced Shou Al' Almihr alone, across a hedge,
at "The Sludge Hole of Balpour." As for Millicent,
the Burlington Arcade had ruined her. She would
never be anything, now, but a shopper.

"Three of spades," Millicent said nervously. She
was nervous not only because she was new to the Colony but because she was having an affair with Safhir,
her houseboy. The house was tiny and Safhir was everywhere. Begun in territoriality, the relationship had
dwindled into passion. Safhir was a tall, well-built
birch of a boy whose loincloth was scribbled over with
poems. Though Millicent loved her husband, "Porky"
Carterhalf, he had become careless in his eating habits,

and, consequently, her love was streaked with lightning flashes of loathing. At the next table, Millicent noticed, a gentleman was writing furiously. "Who's that?" she queried Fitzroy. Fitzroy glanced over casually. "Oh, *him*. It's Willie Maugham, the scribbler. Can you imagine a grown man writing *stories?*" He snorted in disgust. "Did you bid?"

Millicent repeated herself—not for the first time.

"Two of hearts," Fitzroy responded coldly. He was known as the best bridge player between Cairo and Khartoum, an area which did not, unfortunately, include India. His wife, Mary, a fey petite blonde, had died the spring before after consuming a forwarded selection from the Fruit-of-the-Month Club. Fitzroy had been inconsolable, though his concubine, Teneeta the Wine Slob, still lived in the little cabin he had erected for her at the edge of his property. Some said that Teneeta had placed a curse on Mary Fitzroy; others that Mary had died from monsoon poisoning. Madeline Cumberland, the social arbiter of the Colony, had said in one of her witty asides, "Sex is to Mary Fitzroy as the thermos bottle is to ice." If Fitzroy had heard her, he would have killed her with one blow of his huge hands, from which little red hairs sprang up. Madeline Cumberland was drinking herself to death because her favorite son, Reginald Cumberland, KCB, had been converted to Shintoism on an overnight hike.

"I pass," Millicent said lamely, as tea was announced in the fan-cooled loggia that served as a cardroom. Who would have guessed that, six months later, she would stumble across Fitzroy at a jahda detoxification center just outside New Delhi?

WOLFGANG AMADEUS MOZART

"I won't play," he said, and stood there in his velveteen doublet, tense and troubled, a small figure set against the seemingly vast background of the empty auditorium. He was five and had just completed the first six *Woodwind Quintets* (K. 348–371). (Köchel's habit of giving extra numbers to the pieces he *likes* has not

made the musicologist's task any the less formidable!)
The boy was exhausted. It had been one *schloss* after
another.

Leopold, his father, said, "Wolfgang, what is the
matter with you?"

"I can't reach the keys when I sit down," Wolfgang
replied.

"Is *that* all!" Leopold sighed with relief. "Termagant!"—he addressed their manager—"either lower the
stool or cut off the legs of the instrument."

"I can't," Termagant protested. "It's a glass piano."

Many Sacher tortes had been consumed the evening
before in honor of the Emperor's name day. It was 9:00
A.M. and half of Vienna was still asleep. What peltings
with cake there had been! What drag races through the
Vienna woods! In their attempt to wake each other up,
the Viennese had committed the ultimate atrocity:
they had allowed commerce to grind to a halt. A drizzle
had settled over the city, ruining who knows what
quantities of pastry! Mozart gazed silently into space
for a moment, and then, standing up, launched into the
haunting melody that begins the andante movement
of the *Seventh Piano Concerto* (K. 395). It was to have
its premiere that night. At the end of the rehearsal,
the entire orchestra got up and applauded Mozart to
the man, except for the harpist, a transsexual.

At the evening performance, Emperor Albert himself occupied the State Box. With him was the infa-
mous Serbian police-spy, Countess Rimini, rumored
to be his mistress. (The Empress had pleaded cholera.)
Addicted to costumes, Countess Rimini was got up as
a rubber plant.

After the concert, the Emperor, who was not without
his sensitive side, came up to the composer. "Mozart,

you've done it again!" In tears, he handed Wolfgang a check for 3,000 groschen.

3,000 *groschen* for the *Seventh Piano Concerto* when Mozart had expected 5,000 *florins!* He was desperately short of cash. He had secretly entered Vienna's Annual Baking Contest (Toddler's Division) and had spent a fortune on imported mocha. He was about to protest, but the press of his admirers separated him from the Emperor.

Leopold came to the rescue. "Could you double it, Emperor?" he shouted over the heads of the crowd. But the Emperor turned aside, overcome by emotion. Wolfgang noticed that one of Countess Rimini's leaves was taking down everything they said.

ANNA PAVLOVA

Seeing her inimitable Swan, few would imagine the grisly sight of her backstage, after the performance, tearing huge hunks of steak from the bone as she devoured the hand-picked sirloins with a cry. Washed down by assistants, she nimbly danced out again for yet another curtain call. St. Petersburg could never get enough of her. All diamond-hard delicacy, all feathery tension on stage, she was like a wild cannibal off. Such are the paradoxes of metabolism. To Vladimir, the stage manager, her inconsistency, her changeability only made his passion for her the more intense. "Eat, *eat*," he would say, in Russian, while he fed her the almost-raw steak. And she would look at him coldly with a cross, icy detachment, as if he did not exist. She had made the mistake of letting him "take" her after an overexcited performance of *Giselle*, and they had begun one of those do-or-die physical attachments—recoil and temptation on her part, slavishness fraught with violence on his—that do not bode well. A provincial too swiftly plunged into the decadence of St. Petersburg, Vladimir had not had time to allow the vinegar of his personality to age into wine.

"Tonight," he whispered to her hoarsely. "In the little closet behind your dressing room. In thirty minutes. Or I will kill you!" He meant it, too.

"I dine with Baron Korzybski tonight," she countered airily, and tearing another piece of meat from Vladimir's hands, she abruptly left.

Pavlova was temperamentally limited, yet the gauge of her emotional barometer registered every nuance between fury and rage. After slapping her dresser, Masha, she shouted, "Get out, graceless Georgian hag!" and, for the first time in years, dressed herself. Naturally she made a few mistakes. Like putting her boots on backwards. She and the Baron were to dine at St. Petersburg's smartest restaurant, SauerCroat, an intimate place of expensive gloom that featured the best goose in Russia. "I'm still hungry," she moued to the dressing-room mirror as she threw three strands of diamonds around her exquisite neck. Carelessly, she allowed a fourth to drop to the floor. Her trained Russian Wolfhound, Neeki, carefully put it back in its jewelbox.

There was a knock on the door. "Another telegram

from Diaghilev, Great One." It was Masha, who knew Pavlova too well to take offense at her insults.

"Throw it into the sewer," Pavlova cried. "I do not dance *moderne* for heem."

At that instant, Vladimir bounded into the room, his eyes the silver-gray of a gun barrel. He glared at her. "Your thirty minutes are up," he said.

"Go, Masha," Pavlova muttered. "Tell the Baron I will be down in a minute."

But in that minute, Pavlova and Vladimir danced with the gods in that eternal Eden only two passionate creatures who have plumbed each other's bodies to the depths can know.

MARCEL PROUST

Paris threatened to become as parched as overburned toast, promised with its aromas of charcoal, the broiling pit, and the quotidian oven, the worst heatwave in its history as a recompense for the delightful weather of the past winter, and yet, in spite of the heat, though Marcel wore his greatcoat and underneath that the camel's hair, the lambskin, four closely-woven shirts, one flannel, three pairs of underwear, the penultimate peau de soie, the ultimate silk, and thirty scarves that Celeste had carefully wound around his body so that he resembled somewhat a mummy prepared for a sarcophagus, a mummy, however, sitting straight up, the leather gloves tightly fitting over the cashmere gloves beneath and those over the custom-made cotton ones below, Egyptian cotton being the only fabric he could tolerate, now, next to his hands for reasons that still proved mysterious to his doctors, while remaining imperviously non-allergenic to wool, the most common epidermal allergic substance of all, he found himself shivering and albeit he had had the surrounding countryside cleared for a quarter of a mile in every direction, not a flower, bush, vine, tree, or weed remained standing, each single representative of greenery or blossom having been meticulously uprooted before he'd even considered stepping out of the apartment at 44 rue Hamelin, he sniffed, ominously, the faintest trace of scent on the air—pollen? it was unmistakably pollen—after he'd gone to all that trouble, his servants poking about in parks and alleyways, the rough, good-natured waiters of the café, the finest peasant types France had to offer, rushing hither and yon in their colorful, striped waistcoats to rip up yet another re-calcitrant petunia, another reluctant privet, a pine tree, coy with refusal and heavy with dirt, having added more than its share to the dusty scene, so he had been told, for, of course, the uprooting had taken place three days ago, time enough indeed, in the ordinary run of things, to have given the dust time to settle, to have allowed the traces of nature's unconscious, and, from a viewpoint not inconsistent with the Darwinian, dogged methods of reproduction to fade out of the air, and to bury forever in the harmless graveyard of the common earth their persistent and malevolent perfumes so harmful to the asthmatic, the sinusitic, and the flushed, nevertheless a certain ambiguity clouded the issue not only because Celeste had perhaps wound the scarves just a bit too tight this time, but because Alfredteen's cruel, yet delicate, androgynous eyes, so reminiscent of the deepest ponds of Normandy, glimpsed as they now were across the black sea of the café table, the firm peninsula of the jaw undercutting the suggestion of velvet faintly lining the upper lip, the skin of a beauty rivaled only by the camelia, damask not being fine enough, nor even the hothouse peach, might have had something to do with it.

CAMILLE SAINT-SAËNS

It wasn't easy, putting all the bones together, but Camille, obsessed by his masterpiece, *Danse Macabre*, knew that unless he could find a fibula by the weekend, the score would not be finished in time for the concert at the Palais Royale. And here was another femur! That's all there seemed to be—femurs!

"What's happening to the French cadaver, Loti?" he asked his friend. Loti, who had a degree in skeletonology, had done most of the digging.

"Like everything," Loti replied, "the quality goes down." And he quoted a popular poem of the day, *"Tout que va/ Va lá-bas."*

A raven shrieked in the distance.

"What's that?" Camille asked, shivering. The hothouse of Paris was his milieu. They were miles from *any* city, now.

"Camille," Loti said, "I have something to tell you. Since I've done most of the digging, I want my name on the score when the work's performed. Hyphenated. 'Loti-Saint-Saëns.' "

Camille looked at his old friend from the lycée with disbelief.

"Loti," he cried, "you cannot mean it!"

"I mean it, all right," Loti said. "All these years, tagging along after you, listening to what a great man you are. 'Camille is a genius,' " he mocked. "Well, that's all over. This is illegal, all this digging up of corpses . . ."

"But it's for Art . . ." Camille began.

"Rot!" Loti exploded. "I've walked in your shadow

long enough, Camille. I want to be minor in my own right."

And they would have come to blows if the Franco-Prussian War hadn't started at precisely that moment. A portable radio on a passing horse conveyed the terrible news. Still, neither of them guessed that in three months all of Europe would be convulsed by the tragic sound of artillery. It would drown out not only the music of *Danse Macabre* but sounds of a more robust nature as well.

Under the impact of the news, the old friends—rancor forgotten—embraced.

Loti broke away first.

"But Camille," he said, frightened, holding his friend at arm's length. "You're all *bones!*"

SAPPHO

She had the day off, the whole day, and, with a sigh, she rose from the bed, contented, in a way, though what, she asked herself, was contentment, really, when so much of what she had once taken for granted seemed, now, fragmentary, illusive, disjunctive? The blue Aegean made a slight purring noise against the white rocks. The blue of the sky was a sharper blue, as if the stars, put out by the light, were hiding behind a scrim, or trying—so she fancied—to invent a new method of making fire, but making it discreetly, with an inner reserve that only increased the intensity of its flame, an effect she had been trying for in the poems. Had she succeeded? Did they really have that stonelike, endlessly durable, obdurate luminescence that shone like a wick dipped in oil behind the finest screen of glasslike mica? How hard she had worked for purity! Yes, for sanctity! How hard she had tried to transform the experiences of the senses into an enduring poem, each stanza as finely chiseled as the face she now saw reflected back from the pool she gazed into, her eyes wet almonds striped by the runnels made by the slight wind, the fine, taut tent of her flesh supported by the delicate trellis of the architecture of her bones—a face not to be forgotten, once seen. She heard a sound behind her, back in the house. M. was waking.

About M. she had mixed feelings. Ever since they had met, some premonition of disaster lay, like a hidden ember, in the burning coals of her happiness. Could people so different ever truly love each other? Could a personality formed by a life of fishing ever meld with one to whom poetry was its single scruple and example? The faint odor of mackerel let her know that, up, M. was approaching her from behind, about to surprise her yet once more with a sodden, ambiguously motivated, morning embrace.

"Working?" M. asked, fishily.

Sappho's eyes took in the surrounding seacoast.

"I ruin these shores against my fragments," she said.

The line sounded vaguely familiar, even to M.

AUGUSTIN EUGÈNE SCRIBE

(A recently discovered notebook makes it clear that, at the time of his death, Scribe was working on a completely new form of drama—the one- or two-line play. Several examples are offered below. They have been translated by the compiler. WARNING: These plays are fully protected by copyright law and permission and fees must be granted and assigned for their performance.)

COUNTDOWN FOR RENÉE

*A furnished apartment in the
Bastille.*

RENÉE AUBERJON
Robespierre has been treating me shamefully.

GLORIA
How awful for you, Renée.

(Curtain)

* * * *

THE CATALONIAN BLUNDER

*A terrace overlooking Bar-
celona.*

RODRIGO
Here, you are happy, Alice?

ALICE
Happy? In *Spain?* With *you?*

(Curtain)

* * * *

ARISTOCRATIC HEIRS

A salon outside Nice. On ball-
room chairs, on a diagonal,
stage right, twelve bishops.
On ballroom chairs, on a di-
agonal, stage left, twelve trea-
sury officials.

TALLEYRAND
(Leaning forward) And *then?*

(Curtain)

* * * *

DESERT APPRENTICES

Outside a pancake house in
Syria.

FIRST TRAVELER
How would you like a Syrian pancake?

SECOND TRAVELER
You can't be serious?

(Curtain)

* * * *

METHYLATED SPIRITS

A hospital corridor in Costa Rica.

NURSE
You are no longer sterile, Dr. Conchito.

DR. CONCHITO
It is a great day for Costa Rica, my friend.

(Curtain)

* * * *

MARY WOLLSTONECRAFT SHELLEY

"Still asleep, Percy Bysshe?" she asked softly. The bedroom held the light from the hills; dawn was rising rapidly. Her candle dripped a bit of wax onto his magnificent hair, but the slow suspiration of his breath—musical and cadenced, as if, even asleep, he were composing a poem—made her heart stir. But she had work to do, work she could not let even *him* know of. For she was tampering with life itself, up in the attic. She had forbidden anyone to come near it, pretending that she was repairing her "dolls," and in a funny way—she laughed—she *was*.

Outside, it was cold. Stone-castle cold, she said to herself, taking the broad steps quickly, until she reached the top of the north tower. There he was, standing in the doorway, an extension cord wrapped around his left ankle. Behind him, the tubes bubbled and the electrodes spit their bluish sparks.

"What are you do . . . ?"

"Ughffph," the monster said.

She realized she'd made the head too small in relation to the body. But synthetic flesh wasn't as easy to get, these days, as people imagined. She'd had to do with bits and pieces. He looked a little like a protoplasmic patchwork quilt.

He tried to take her hand. She recoiled.

He grabbed a pad and pencil and wrote, "Oi . . . luff . . . ooo . . ."

How ghastly! And yet how miraculous! He had learned to read and write overnight! All by himself! And she had made him up out of . . . wholecloth.

"I don't think we'd be . . ."

"Unghk," he said, the faint blush of anger beginning to douse the patched-up "features" that passed for a "face."

"Would you like some cranberry juice?" she asked, desperate to amuse him while she secretly filled a hypodermic needle with 1,000 ccs. of phenobarbital, her favorite drug.

"Suture . . . self," he said. The remark left no narrow chink for a rejoinder. She tried.

"A walk? How about a walk?"

He smiled, ivory showing through the integuments

she had stretched above the few bits of whalebone she had been able to purloin.

"Ye . . . ess . . . wor . . . war . . . auk."

Where could they go? she wondered. There was a pounding at the door. My God! Could it be Percy Bysshe? If he found out she'd been "experimenting" again, it would kill him.

"Just one moment, please," she said, trying to shove the monster back into the darkness of the attic.

"Get back into a recess . . . back! . . . back!" Mary whispered hoarsely.

The monster looked at her. "That's easier Sade than Donne . . ."

Even in this intolerable moment of panic, Mary could not resist a tiny rush of pride. Whatever she had created, it was far more literate than she had guessed . . .

———

GERTRUDE STEIN

Humming Satie's latest while she dressed, she became a little misty-eyed when she thought over the guest list. In spite of her eminence as a Paris hostess, she was still basically a celebrity-struck little girl from Baltimore, although her massive build might lead one to think otherwise, being more peasant than puissant. She had been working on *The Making of an American* secretly in the closet for some time. Somehow she didn't want to share it with anyone yet, not even her nearest and dearest. *This* book was to be truly hers and hers only alone lonely alone a lone lonely hers alone.

But the doorbell was insistently ringing, and putting a last touch on the oversized skirt and blouse Balenciaga had personally whipped up for her, gratis, for reasons best known to them both, she opened the door leading into the courtyard. There they were! "Pablo! Djuna! Janet! Henri! Virgil! Marcel! Claude! Ernest! Kay!" And behind them she could see Mallarmé, Valéry, Eliot, Ravel, Apollinaire, Paul Klee, Duchamp, Claudel, Gide, Mauriac, Léger, Max Brod, Kafka, Max Ernst, Mayakovsky, Cocteau, Marais, Malraux, Giraudoux, the two Cone girls, and Gloria, all crowding to get in.

"One at a time, please," she said, irritated, her rationality cutting through the scene of near-panic that threatened to turn the thirteenth-century courtyard, with all its charm, into a charnel house. It was May, and Paris had never looked lovelier. The chestnut blossoms had unburdened themselves of their snowy cargo. The effect was an angelic, aerial parade.

Later, over coffee, Pablo said, "I want to show you my latest, Gert," and brought out the famous painting, *Figure Seated in Wicker Chair*. At the same moment, all-done-in from having tested the recipe of the hashish fudge yet again, Alice lurched into the room. "I hope you haven't been *guzzling*," Gertrude said, with a look that spoke volumes. "You know everyone," she finished curtly.

"Everyone but Gloria," Alice said.

But Gertrude had turned her attention back to the painting. "It's beautiful, Pablo. Thank you."

"I just wanted to *show* it to you," he said, nervously.

But she had already clasped the frame in an iron grip.

"Have to take it back. Finishing touches," Pablo muttered, uneasily.

"Oh, Pablo," Gertrude laughed. "Whatever do you mean?"

Unseen by the others, a silent struggle took place between them. And though the rest of the evening was a typical, brilliant salon-type affair for which the house had become notorious (marred only by the Cone girls' attempt to slip two small paintings, as well as bits of food, into the capacious pockets of their homemade mackintoshes), for Pablo Picasso it was another losing battle.

PETER ILICH TCHAIKOVSKY

Another note from Madame von Meck: "Petroosha: I was watching you through the binoculars and your green tie has a stain on it. Also, you were leaning *very* close to Marina Pavlovna Schoulbetsky in the carriage. Why were you out at all? You wrote me you were working on your symphony. Is that the way you work on your symphony? This month I send 1,000 roubles instead of 5,000. Do not break my heart. M."

That bitch, Peter said to himself, as he waited for Count Kropkin to dress. Am I never to have a moment's peace? He was getting tired of Kropkin—all

Black Sea bonelessness and Crimea mincings. Later, sitting at the piano, he banged out the theme from the *Second Piano Concerto*. He was upset. Life was sad, sad, *sad*. But was it not an old axiom that the artist must suffer?

He had a sudden inspiration. Not a pig ballet but a bird ballet! He rushed over to his writing desk and changed "Swine" to "Swan." *Swan Lake*. Of course! The whole thing was falling into place. Lakes. Glass. Ice. He started to drink seriously between four and five. Why not answer the note, and say what he felt for once? Sobbing a bit—he had thought of Glinka, Glinka the *success*—he went back to the desk.

"My dear Patroness: I will *not* be down in the neighboring hut you call a chateau for the weekend. I am *deep* in work." Here he laughed, and emptied a bottle of Circassian Brandy. "I will of course miss being under *constant* surveillance, *watched* through binoculars, and *followed* by paid spies. Otherwise, I will miss *nothing*. Please send me the other 4,000 roubles. The dedication of the symphony hangs in the balance. Poor as ever—Peter."

To make matters worse, a telegram arrived from Moussorgsky: "Do you want to be one of The Five or not? Make up your mind."

They were all trying to torture him! All!

He was found lying in the gutter in front of the Tolstoy Cantina by his old teacher, Anton Rubinstein, and his French wife.

As they helped him home, Madame Rubinstein turned to her husband and said, *"C'est dommage . . . mais il est très sympathique."*

Rubinstein thought for a moment. "Not *sympa*thique, my dear. *Pathé*tique."

JAN VAN EYCK

"Where's the lamb? And the adorers?" Van Eyck angrily asked.

The burgher, a clairvoyant, was flustered.

"Well, you see, it's this way . . . Van Dyck . . ."

"Eyck."

"I mean Jan . . ."

"Jan *Van,* you fool."

"Well, Dyck . . . excuse me, Eyck . . . the lamb didn't come."

"The lamb didn't come?" Van Eyck couldn't believe his ears. "What does *that* mean?"

"Last night, half of them went over to Holland," the burgher said.

"And the other half?"

"*They* went over to Burgundy."

"Are you suggesting an insurrection of *lambs?*" Van Eyck demanded.

"No, but I *am* suggesting a dichotomy."

Van Eyck tapped his foot, sheathed in velvet, against the parquetry.

"There are no lambs to be had for love nor money," the burgher muttered.

"*Or* money," Van Eyck corrected him. He detested the incorrect usage of "nor."

"And the adorers?" he went on.

"They say a demon is at work. And they . . . well, they's afraid, Van . . ." The burgher was lapsing into the vernacular from nervousness.

"*Mr.* Eyck," Van Eyck emphasized. Would this fellow never stop being familiar?

"Well, could you get me something in its place? The lamb, I mean," the painter continued.

"Such as, sir?"

"I don't know . . . Something analogous to the original."

The burgher hesitated. "Lamb chops, sir?"

A Flemish pause ensued. "Get out. Get *out*. Get OUT!" Van Eyck shouted.

The burgher ran out of the house.

Thus Van Eyck's achievement is all the more remarkable in that, due to a deficiency of lambs, his famous painting, "The Adoration of the Lamb," rather than being drawn from life had to be completely made up.

OSCAR WILDE

"Bon mots, among intimates, are the cablegrams of the desert," Oscar said, his finger still firmly on the pulse of the epigram. Bosie was being retrograde and piggish. He hadn't the faintest notion of the hideous conflict that seethed in his friend's breast. Oscar had secretly finished the first act of *The Importance of Being Earnest* that very afternoon and was torn with doubt. Cucumber sandwiches? Watercress sandwiches? The whole scene would stand or fall on his ultimate decision. The two of them were holed up at the Cadogan, their secret summer retreat. Who would think of looking for them in *London*? In *August*?

Alfred Lord Douglas's handsome profile was silhouetted against the window. Behind him, a judicious square of lime, Sloane Park, gave off its summerlike perfume, a mixture of coal dust and acacia.

"This bag," Bosie said. He so much preferred the Connaught.

"Hotels are the greenhouses of the dead," Oscar said, sipping a Scotch and soda. "Another, Bosie?" There must be no *crise* tonight.

"Could there *be* another Bosie?" Bosie asked, coyly. "I'll have one, yes," he said, accepting the proffered drink without a "Thank you."

"Everyone's going to be at Timothy's tonight. Except us, of course. We'll be here, at this little mousetrap of an hotel."

"Society is the press gang of the insecure," said the eminent playwright.

"Oh, for God's sake, Oscar, *can* it," Bosie replied, in a rare show of manliness. "How do I look?" he continued. He knew very well that he looked very well.

"Well," Oscar said. Actually, Bosie was getting older and fatter—one doesn't stay eighteen forever. "Maud Fortescue-Pringle is throwing the biggest do of the year after the theatre tonight. Exactly the same people will be at Maud's as at Timothy's."

"*Two* parties and we'll only be at *one*," said Bosie, with the petulance of a child. There had been a series of growing difficulties between them. He glanced at an envelope on the table.

"Who is this Alfred Gide, anyway?"

"André," Oscar returned. "The most interesting new novelist on the Continent. If you'd only read, instead of partying . . ."

"Playwriting is the last resort of the uninvited," Bosie interrupted, knowing full well the dreadful import of his words.

So, Oscar thought, the honeymoon is over.

BENEPPO
OR, THE SQUID OF ST. ANDREW

(AN OPERA IN FOUR ACTS)

ACT I

Mikhail is failing in his study. And in his studies, too. Maria, under the false impression that he is the valedictorian of his graduating class and treasurer of the Victorian Club, sings of her pride in her young husband's accomplishments, "Io Voca Tenabalae Puisso" ("My Heart Grows Tiny at Thy Command"). Mikhail emerges, covered with dust, to tell of his long struggle to finish his thesis on Thomas Love Peacock, "Questo Avia Pluma di Cielo?" ("Who Cares Whether Peacocks Are Colored?"). He is about to leave Naples to join his regiment for night maneuvers when a piece of paper falls out of his pocket. Maria reads it and, learning the truth, sinks to her knees for the heartbreaking aria "Pret Buffa Augmi" ("I Am Augmented by a Supposed Rebuff"). She is interrupted, near the end, by the German instructor, Loder. He has been courting Maria, though he is secretly married to Mikhail's former girlfriend, Lucia de Zenza, who has gone temporarily mad. It is a time of political trouble, and the Duke of Turin, also in love with Lucia, has been neglecting his duties by spending too many hours at the asylum, arguing and haggling with the receptionist. This has enraged his officers, one of whom, Aristo, sings of the glories of the military life—"Camp Militaria Mio Nuggia?" (What Can Compare to Breakfast Among Guns?")—

and of his love for Maria and her pet dog, Maria 2. Because Mikhail's college is housed in an outbuilding of the madhouse, all converge on the asylum as the set slowly changes in the gathering dusk and we hear the Gay Chorus of Naples singing through the windows "Quello Macho de Plus Commedia Quandario" ("What Foolish Puzzles Men Become"). Snow begins to fall. All enter the building as Lucia, who has escaped through an air-conditioning duct, emerges, carrying her newborn baby, Vicenzo. The handsome but mentally twisted gatekeeper, Mario, tells Lucia he will take her to America if she abandons Vicenzo. "Never!" she cries as the three of them struggle in the snow, and the curtain falls.

Act II

Against the shadowy background of what appears to be a château but is in reality the headquarters of the Meat Packers Union of Lyons, Astride is discovered in her kimono weeping under a beech tree. Her anklet has fallen into the pig wallow. It has been her one link with reality from the day her twin sister, Craquelure, died of overexposure. Astride has subsisted on nothing but canapés ever since, and sings, with little cries, "Est-ce que Je Suis Moi, Moi-Même, ou Quelqu'une Autre?" ("Am I I, Me, Myself, or Somebody Else Entirely?"). Prince Bayeux, bilingual from birth, gallops in on his bay calling "Which?" ("Ou?"), and the horse executes a sensational piaffe to convey his status. A leaf falls, informing Astride that the Emperor is dying of imperial languor, and Astride and Bayeux hurry back to the palace as the forest slides away to reveal a vast chamber. The Emperor is lying on a chaise, attended by his aged courtesan, Bibi. In one hand she holds a tiny white flag on which the word "Drinks" is emblazoned, and sings "Non Perles Demarque la Robe Boison du Soir" ("No pearls Set Off the Cocktail Dress of Night"). Looking into a crystal ball, she tells Astride that the anklet is slowly being nibbled to pieces by sows, while Astride weeps helplessly at the foot of the Emperor's bed. As the Emperor passes away, a raven flies over, a horse neighs in the distance, and a floor-length mirror cracks, interrupting Bayeux, who has been standing in front of it arguing the merits of bilateral symmetry. As the light slowly fades, an image of the anklet crosses the stage and lingers in the cracked mirror while the characters stand transfixed. An old, blind serf enters, bearing a tray of cookies, stumbles, and the curtain falls.

Act III

Losan, whose Sacred Earrings have fallen into the hands of Grafner, makes a compact with the Pygmies to destroy the earth if Sielford should emerge from the forest without having made a mortal union. Sielford, unwittingly, has allowed the Unfner Mass to sink below the forest floor, and the gods, once his protectors, have turned against him. He mourns his fate in the basso *glanzstück* "Mein Haus nahm dich Tranen Floth" ("Flute Training Is Forbidden Near This House"). Meanwhile, Erdra, who has fought the dragon, Sluth, for weeks, stands in a clearing asking the gods for help. Because of her relationship with Sielford, they refuse. She sings, in her despair, "Wildes Gesschlecht ihn Gerufen" ("Wind Burdens Me with Its Rough Works"). Her son by a former union, Halbrecht, has been exiled from Valhalla for bartering pine chips and has gone to Loder's hut to tell of his woes. There, he swears eternal vengeance on the Mother of the Earrings, Celia: "Celia, Haus Hutetallen Mir?" ("Celia, You Little Cheat, Where Are My Earrings?"). Groten, suspended in a dehydrated state for a thousand years for giving the magic apple to Münster, is released by a swarm of midges, as Loder, having fallen in love with her in her desiccated state, watches her emergence into mortal form with rapture: "Mein Blut Steigt zu Schaum!" ("Oh, How My Blood Rises Into Foam!"). Groten, weary from her ordeal, asks for a drink of mead, the one gift it is forbidden the gods to give, and instantly becomes dehydrated again for another thousand years. Beside himself with grief, Loder rushes through the forest, only to be ambushed by the Pygmies, who have borne the Sacred Earrings through the woods and, on seeing Loder, thrown them into a well. He is brought to the Cave of the Underworld, where he recognizes in a ray of light Groten's other form, that of a spindle. As the Pygmies sing "Trost, Sieh Neue Bilder Sind Erklart" ("Solace, Behold New Images Are Bid"), the Unfner Mass rises through the forest floor and unearthly music issues from the well. Losan, Erdra, Grafner, and Sielford emerge from the shadows of the trees. As they embrace in a happy reunion, Sluth descends from the sky in the form of a bird and, turning once more into a dragon, threatens to destroy them all in "Einschnung" ("A Sick Illusion Blinds Your Will"), as the curtain falls.

ACT IV

Lucia, disguised as a sailor, and now a major in marine biology, arrives in Sicily on the *largetto*. She sings of her love for the puppet, Pietro, whom she has adored since childhood. Admitting, in agitated half-*sprech-stimme,* that she has feigned madness in order to avoid the staggering medical fees rendered by her pediatrician—"Ein Kreinkeit il de Plus Malade" ("The Sick Get Sicker When They Get the Bill")—she wonders how her son Vicenzo grew up in no time to be an eighteen-year-old tenor dabbling in black-market plastics. A funeral takes place for Maria and the Duke of Turin, killed by sipping watered-down espresso: "Caffè Morta—Non?" ("Death from Coffee—Is It Truly Unexpected?"). Aristo, pretending to be lost, in preparation for his entering a nearby Capuchin monastery, keeps asking Grafner for directions—"Kunst du il Piallo?" ("Do You Know Anything?")—until Beneppo, a well-built scholar, and Losan appear to explain that the Unfner Mass was only an optical illusion projected on a scrim by the revenant Craquelure to ferret out the "good ones." A vision of St. Andrew appears, as Craquelure's ghost rises from the prompter's box to sing "Va-t-en, Les Dieux Malheurs d'Amour" ("Disport Elsewhere, Vile Deities of Love"). Mikhail bursts onstage left, bearing a life-size likeness of Thomas Love Peacock wearing the Sacred Earrings, and a squid (the dead Sluth) is brought onstage right by Astride and Bayeux (symbolized by two dimly lit Ping-Pong balls) as the Fisherman's Chorus rejoices in the restoration of peace to the island: "Les Hommes il Mare Vino Macht" ("Male Calmness Makes the Sea Like Wine"). Curtain.

POSSIBLY RICARDO

"Maynard Keynes (is) . . . with Smith, Marx,
and possibly Ricardo, one of the three or
four gratest economists who ever lived."
—John Kenneth Galbraith,
The New York Review of Books,
November 22, 1984

SCENE: *A dressing room at the Teatro Galicia in Barcelona, scantily furnished with a couch, a few chairs, a makeup table, mirror, and fan. A small Goya hangs over the escritoire.*

INTERVIEWER: You read what Mr. Galbraith said?

RICARDO: (With a deprecatory wave of the hand) Agh!
Too kind!

INT: I'm ashamed to say I never heard of you. It took
me days to find out who you were, and where. . . .
What a trip!

RIC: Next time, ship. Much nicer.

INT: But, tell me, what does Galbraith mean? What,
for instance, is the name of your theory? I mean
supply-side, split-side, sideline, class struggle . . . ?

RIC: Oh, no. No. I have never been to—what you call
it?—high school. (He struggles with his flamenco straps

and shoes.) *Blasfemas!* Excuse. (He smiles.) I have amassed great fortune.

INT: But still you dance . . .

RIC: Ah, but that is the point. Mr. Galbraith must be referring to The Peseta Trick. I do not mean to be *inmodesto* when I say it is truly my invention. I put peseta under one foot, and as I become inflame with the rhythm, the passion, the speed and heat melts under the sole. . . .

INT: Yes?

RIC: The peseta. And with the other foot, on which is especially stamped the design of a gold doubloon . . .

INT: I thought they were obsolete!

RIC: I revive. I fire the piece of metal and make gold. Gold is obsolete? (He laughs.) From peseta to doubloon. Of course, it takes great skill. . . . Each penny a dollar. . . .

(He is interrupted by a knock on the door and a voice calling, "Five minutes, Senor Ricardo.")

RIC: (Continuing) At home, all night, I dance, dance! I make thousands! Millions!

INT: But isn't it illegal?

RIC: No, no. Counter*feit* is illegal. Not counter*foot*. No law to *hacer* peseta into doubloon. And no tax!

(Ricardo puts on black shoes, white shirt, the para-phernalia of the flamenco. An orchestra starts up in the background.)

INT: You know, I don't even know your first name. Karl Marx, Adam Smith, and . . .

RIC: Here is my card. (Shyly) And here is a doubloon for you.

INT: Oh, thank you. (Reading) Ricardo Ricardo . . .

(A voice from behind the door shouts: "Curtain go-ing up!")

RIC: I must leave. *Muchas gracias.* Goodbye. *Adios.* And *muchas felicidades* on your money, money, mon-ey, money . . .

(Door opens. Wild splash of light. Ricardo runs out to great applause. The door closes.)

INT: (To audience, ambiguously) So that was Ricardo! (The light dawns. He gets up and slowly walks toward the closet.) I . . . wonder . . . if . . . he . . . has . . . another . . . pair . . . of . . . shoes. . . .

(Curtain)

* * * *

THE ULTIMATE DIARY

(Further Daily Jottings of a Contemporary Composer)

Monday

Drinks here. Picasso, Colette, the inevitable Cocteau, Gide, Valéry, Ravel, and Larry. Chitchat. God, how absolutely dull the Great can be! I know at least a hundred friends who would have given their eyeteeth just to have had a *glimpse* of some of them, and there I was bored, incredible lassitude, *stymied*. Is it me? Is it them? Think latter. Happened to glance in mirror before going to bed. Am more beautiful than ever.

Tuesday

Horrible. After organ lesson at C's, he burst into tears and confessed that he loved me. Was mad about me, is how he put it. I was embarrassed. I respect him, he is a great *maître* and all that, but how could I reciprocate when I, myself, am so involved with L? I tried to explain. He said he thought it would be better if we discontinued our lessons. How am I ever going to learn to play the organ? Came home upset. Finished *Barcarolles, Gigue, Danse Fantastique,* and *Cantata*. Writing better than ever. Careful of self-congratulations. So somebdy said. John Donne? Fresh mushrooms. Delicious.

Wednesday

Drunk at the dentist's. He removed a molar, and cried when I said it hurt. *Très gentil.* I think he has some feeling for me. The sky was like a red blister over the Dome. Streaks of carmine suffused the horizon. Sometimes I wonder if I shouldn't have been a writer. Drunk as I was, I caught a glimpse of myself in a bakery window. No wonder so many people love me!

THURSDAY

Arletty said something profound at lunch. "The trouble with homosexuals is that they like men." She sometimes gets to the heart of the matter with all her superficiality. She is leaving M. Talked and talked about it. I found my attention wandering, and kept seeing the unfinished pages of the *Symphony*. It is a great hymn to world peace, a kind of apotheosis of calmness, though it has a few fast sections. Drank a lot, and can't remember much after lunch. Woke up in Bois. Think something happened. But what? To relieve depression, dyed my hair again. Must say it looks ravishing. *Ravissant.*

FRIDAY

Calls from Mauriac and Claudel. Why don't they leave me alone?

FRIDAY, LATER

Larry back from Avignon. Seems changed. Felt vague feeling of disgust. To camouflage, worked all day and finished *Pavane, Song Cycles,* and *Sonata.* Dedicated latter—last?—to Princesse de N. She sent me a Russian egg for my name day. How know? Malraux, Auric, Poulenc, and Milhaud dropped by.

SATURDAY

Stravinsky angry with me, he said over phone. I

must never stop working, working. What about sex? L has left. Should I call C? Thinking of it. Press clippings arrived. Is there any other composer under seventeen whose works are being played in every capital of Asia? Matisse said, jokingly at lunch, that I was too beautiful to live. Genius is not a gift; it is a loan.

SATURDAY, LATER

At state banquet for de Gaulle, misbehaved. Slapped his wife in face during coffee. Drunk. Terribly depressed, but am I not also not a little proud? Contrite but haughty, sorry but pleased? Can't remember issue. Something about Monteverdi? Sent her a dozen white roses as apology. The Princesse says I should get out of town for a while. I WILL NOT RUN AWAY! C back. We are both more gorgeous than ever. Finished *War and Peace*. A good book.

SUNDAY

Pneumatique from Mallarmé. I will not answer. C and I had pique-nique. Fell asleep on Seine bank. Dream: Mother in hippopotamus cage, crying. She said, "If music be the feast . . ." and then gobbled up by crowd of angry deer. What mean? Shaken. C bought me drink at Deux Magots. Sweet. Told me he thought there had never been a handsomer man placed on this earth. Forced to agree, after catching tiny glimpse of myself in café window. How often are genius and beauty united? They will hate me when they read this diary, but I tell the truth. How many can say as much?

MONDAY

A name even *I* cannot mention. . . . And he wants

me to spend the summer in Africa with him! C angry. Finished *Concerto Grosso* and *Hymn to the Moon,* for female voices. Something new, a kind of rough susurration, here and there, a darkening of strings. It is raining. Sometimes I think we are more ourselves in wet weather than in dry. Bought linen hat.

TUESDAY

Gertrude, Alice, James, Joyce, Henry Green, Virginia Woolf, Eliot, Laforgue, Mallarmé (all is forgiven!), Rimbaud's nephew, Claudel's niece, Mistinguett, Nadia, Marais, Nijinska, Gabin, and the usual for drinks. I did it with Y in the pantry while the party was going on! Ashamed but exhilarated. I think if THEY knew they would have approved. Finished *Sixty Piano Pieces for Young Fingers.* Potboiler. But one has to live!

WEDNESDAY

Snow. Hideous hangover. Will never drink again. Deli dinner with Henry Miller.

THURSDAY

Half the Opéra-Comique seems to have fallen in love with me. I cannot stand any more importuning. Will go to Africa. How to break with C? Simone de Beauvoir, Simone Signoret, Simone Weil, and Simone Simon for drinks. The didn't get it!

FRIDAY

C left. Am bruised but elated. Dentist. I was right. I wonder if he'll dare send me a bill. *Now,* I mean. Tea with Anaïs. *Enchantant.*

SATURDAY

René Char and Dior for lunch. Interesting. Clothes are the camouflage of the soul. Leave for Africa with X tomorrow. Had fifty tiny Martinis. Nothing happened.

SUNDAY

Barrault, Braque, Seurat, Mayakovski, Honegger, and René Clair saw us off. Very gala. I think I am really in love for the first time. I must say I looked marvellous. Many comments. Wore green yachting cap and cinnamon plus fours. Happy.

WEDNESDAY

Dakar: Tangled in mosquito netting. Getting nowhere with *Chansons d'Afrique*.

SATURDAY

Back in Paris. God, what a fool I've been! Someday I will write down the whole hideous, unbelievable story. Not now, Not when I am so close to it. But I will forget *nothing*. Leaving tonight for Princesse de N's country place. Green trees, green leaves! The piercing but purifying wind of Provence! Or is it Normandy? Packed all afternoon. Long bath, many thoughts. Proust called. . . .

HOWARD MOSS's collection *The Miles Between: New Selected Poems* is being brought out this spring and his *Selected Essays* will be appearing in the fall. A new translation of Valéry's *Le Cimitière Marin* will be coming out in a special edition from The Aralia Press. Mr. Moss received the National Book Award for his *Selected Poems* and more recently a Citation in Poetry from Brandeis University and a National Endowment for the Arts grant. Mr. Moss lives in New York City and East Hampton and is the poetry editor of *The New Yorker.*

EDWARD GOREY's most recent book is *The Tunnel Calamity.* His anthology, *Amphigorey,* was published in 1972; it contains such famous Gorey titles as *The Doubtful Guest, The Curious Sofa,* and *The Listening Attic.*